THE EXTERMINATING ANGEL

The Exterminating Angel

An Opera in Three Acts

Libretto by
TOM CAIRNS
in collaboration with the composer

Based on the screenplay by
Luis Buñuel and Luis Alcoriza

Set to music by
THOMAS ADÈS

FABER *ff* MUSIC

Commissioned by the 2016 Salzburg Festival, the Royal Opera House, Covent Garden,
the Metropolitan Opera New York, and the Royal Danish Opera

The first performance of *The Exterminating Angel* was given in the Haus für Mozart,
Salzburg, by the Salzburger Bachchor and the ORF Radio-Symphonieorchester Wien,
conducted by the composer, on 28 July 2016

Duration: *c.* 115 minutes

Vocal score, full score and orchestral parts available on hire from the publishers

All enquiries relating to *The Exterminating Angel* should be addressed to the
Performance Department, Faber Music Ltd. Bloomsbury House,
74–77 Great Russell Street, London WC1B 3DA

Tel: +44 (0) 2079085311   promotion@fabermusic.com

To buy Faber Music publications or to find out about the full range of titles available
please contact your local music retailer or Faber Music sales enquiries:

Faber Music Limited, Burnt Mill, Elizabeth Way, Harlow, Essex, CM20 2HX, England
Tel: +44 (0)1279 82 89 82 Fax: +44 (0)1279 82 89 83

sales@fabermusic.com   fabermusic.com

CHARACTERS

Lucía, Marquesa de Nobile, hostess – *soprano*
Leticia Maynar, an opera singer – *high coloratura*
Leonora Palma – *mezzo-soprano*
Silvia, Duchess of Ávila, a young widowed mother – *soprano*
Blanca Delgado, pianist, wife of Roc – *mezzo-soprano*
Beatriz, fiancée of Eduardo – *soprano*
Edmundo, Marqués de Nobile, host – *tenor*
Count Raúl Yebenes, explorer – *tenor*
Colonel Álvaro Gómez – *high baritone*
Francisco de Ávila, brother of Silvia – *counter-tenor*
Eduardo, fiancé of Beatriz – *tenor (lyric)*
Señor Russell, elderly man – *bass-baritone*
Alberto Roc, a conductor – *bass-baritone*
Doctor Carlos Conde – *bass*

Julio, a butler – *baritone*
Lucas, a footman – *tenor*
Enrique, a waiter – *tenor*
Pablo, a cook – *baritone*
Meni, a maid – *soprano*
Camila, a maid – *mezzo-soprano*

Padre Sansón – *baritone*
Yoli, a small boy, son of Silvia – *boy treble*

CHORUS (SATB) playing servants, policemen, army, crowd

ACT 1

Bells. A MAN *enters leading some* SHEEP. *He waits.*

SCENE 1

HALLWAY

A luxurious mansion on the Calle de la Providencia. The home of LUCÍA *and Edmundo* NOBILE.
A member of staff, LUCAS, *is putting on his coat and hat. As he hurries off,* JULIO, *the Butler, calls after him.*

JULIO   You! Where d'you think you're going?

LUCAS   For a walk. I won't be long.

JULIO   A walk? We've a dozen people coming for dinner and you're going for a walk?

LUCAS   I wish I didn't have to leave.

JULIO   You're not going anywhere, Lucas!

LUCAS   I have to go!

JULIO   You have to take the coats.

They struggle for a moment. JULIO *relents.*

JULIO   Very well, go! But don't ever set foot in this house again!

LUCAS *stumbles off.*

SCENE 2

KITCHEN

Three LAMBS *stand forlornly under a huge table. A few* STAFF *rush around. Instead of preparing for the guests' arrival, they seem to be leaving their posts, much like* LUCAS.

MENI	Camila, what do we do?
CAMILA	Whatever you want. But soon! I've got to get out of this house.
MENI	But where can we go at this late hour?
CAMILA	I have a friend who'll let me sleep at her house.
ENRIQUE	I will come with you. I'll take you in a taxi, wherever you want to go.
PABLO	You stay right here, Enrique, and wait for me. Madame wants you to serve the *ragoût*.
ENRIQUE	Why does it have to be me that serves the *ragoût*?
PABLO	Because you're a clown.

SCENE 3

HALLWAY

The GUESTS *are arriving for dinner. They are Sr* RUSSELL, RAÚL *Yebenes, Sr Alberto* ROC *and his wife* BLANCA *Delgado,* FRANCISCO *and his sister* SILVIA, LEONORA *Palma,* DOCTOR *Carlos Conde,* COLONEL *Álvaro Gómez,* LETICIA *Maynar, a delicious vamp, and* EDUARDO *and* BEATRIZ, *who are terribly in love.* NOBILE *and* LUCÍA *lead them into the house.*

NOBILE	How strange. Lucas isn't here to take the coats.
COLONEL	Lucas?
LUCÍA	The footman.
NOBILE	Dear friends, please keep your coats. They will take them upstairs. Come in, please.
LUCÍA	Señor Russell, may I present Señora Blanca Delgado.
RUSSELL	Enchanted.
LUCÍA	Colonel Álvaro Gómez.
COLONEL	Enchanted.
LUCÍA	And, of course, her husband, Maestro Alberto Roc!
BLANCA, ROC	
	Enchanted.
NOBILE	Leonora Palma, Silvia, Duchess of Ávila and her brother, Don Francisco.
SILVIA, LEONORA, FRANCISCO, COLONEL, RUSSELL	
	Enchanted.
LUCÍA	Count Yebenes, the explorer . . .
RAÚL (*interrupting*)	
	Raúl.

BEATRIZ *and* EDUARDO *introducing themselves to* RAÚL.

EDUARDO	Eduardo.
BEATRIZ	Beatriz.

LEONORA (*to* BEATRIZ *and* EDUARDO)
Enchanted.

LUCÍA   And the famous Doctor Carlos Conde.

DOCTOR   Enchanted.

LUCÍA, NOBILE
And here she is, Leticia Maynar.

THE REST Enchanted.

MENI *and* CAMILA, *hiding from the guests.*

MENI   They're here! They've already gone inside.

CAMILA   I'm worried about leaving. It isn't right to run off
          like this.

MENI   You should have thought of that before! If you
          don't want to come with me you're free to stay!

CAMILA   But what about our things?

MENI   Not now, we have to hurry. We'll come back for
          them tomorrow.

CAMILA   Tomorrow? They won't let us in the house
          tomorrow. I'll pack very quickly. You can wait
          for me outside.

MENI   No! Leave it! We must leave right away.

MENI, CAMILA
Vamos! Vamos!

A few more SERVANTS *run in from different directions. They all
flee the house. The main door opens on to the driveway again.
The* MAIDS *hide in a panic.*

The GUESTS *are arriving for dinner.* NOBILE *and* LUCÍA *greet everyone warmly.*

NOBILE   How strange! Lucas . . .

COLONEL   Lucas?

LUCÍA   The footman.

NOBILE   . . . isn't here to take the coats. Dear friends, please keep your coats. They will take them upstairs. Come in, please.

LUCÍA   Señor Russell, may I present Señora Blanca Delgado.

RUSSELL   Enchanted.

BLANCA, ROC
          Enchanted.

LUCÍA   Colonel Álvaro Gómez.

COLONEL   Enchanted.

BLANCA, ROC
          Enchanted.

LUCÍA   And, of course, her husband, Maestro Alberto Roc!

COLONEL, RUSSELL
          Enchanted.

NOBILE   Leonora Palma, Silvia, Duchess of Ávila, and her brother, Don Francisco.

SILVIA, LEONORA, FRANCISCO, COLONEL
          Enchanted.

5

LUCÍA   Count Yebenes, the explorer . . .

RAÚL (*interrupting* LUCÍA)
             Raúl.

EDUARDO   Eduardo.

BEATRIZ   Beatriz.

LUCÍA   And the famous Doctor Carlos Conde.

LUCÍA, NOBILE
             And here she is – Leticia Maynar.

ALL (*except* LUCÍA, NOBILE)
             Enchanted.

The GUESTS *disappear into the house.* MENI *and* CAMILA *are*
frozen in horror as another group of anxious SERVANTS *appear*
and make their escape. MENI *and* CAMILA, *too, finally make a run*
for it.

MENI, CAMILA
             Vamos!

                          SCENE 4

DINING ROOM
A large, splendidly laid-out table. The glint of silverware, cut
glass; the glow of candles. NOBILE *and* LUCÍA *are seated at either*
end. Everyone looks ravishing, elegant, rich.

COLONEL   No, I've never tasted it . . .

BLANCA   So although you're the youngest colonel in the army,
             you have never been ambitious for honour and
             glory? You don't want to be a hero!

COLONEL   Blanca! I cannot stand the noise of gunfire.

BLANCA   Ah, but what of the Fatherland?

COLONEL   The Fatherland is nothing but a group of rivers
that flow into the sea.

BLANCA   The sea, which is death!

COLONEL   Death for the Fatherland!

NOBILE *taps on his glass with a spoon and stands.*

LUCÍA   Álvaro, Blanca, I think my husband would like to
say a few words.

NOBILE *raises his glass of champagne.*

NOBILE   To the exquisite evening our friend Leticia has given
us tonight with her stupendous performance as the
virgin bride of Lammermoor.

LETICIA *smiles graciously in acknowledgement.*

ALL (*except* LETICIA)
Leticia.

RAÚL (*aside to* LEONORA)
Bride maybe, but virgin? I don't think so.

SILVIA, FRANCISCO
But that's why we call her *die Walküre*.

RAÚL   *Die Walküre?*

SILVIA   Leticia Maynar.

FRANCISCO *Die Walküre.* We call her that because she is
a savage.

7

SILVIA   A virgin savage.

RAÚL   Virgin? Do you really think so?

FRANCISCO They say she has kept it intact.

SILVIA, FRANCISCO
               But it could be a perversion.

A REPEAT
NOBILE *stands for second toast.*

NOBILE   To the exquisite evening our friend Leticia has given
               us tonight with her stupendous performance as the
               virgin bride of Lammermoor.

LUCÍA *stands.*

LUCÍA   My friends, you must all forgive me for changing
               the natural order of the menu. Tonight we will
               begin with a Maltese *ragoût* which, according to
               island custom, is served as an hors d'oeuvre,
               because it is said to stimulate the appetite. Liver,
               honey and almonds!

ALL   Liver, honey and almonds.

LUCÍA   And with many spices in the sauce!

ALL   . . . many spices in the sauce!

ROC   Delicious! I had it in Capri . . . a concert I
               conducted there a thousand years ago.

ENRIQUE *arrives with a magnificent tray laden with succulent
meats swamped in a savoury sauce. All eyes are on the waiter
who struggles with the huge tray.*

LUCÍA   Here it is! Enter stage left!

FRANCISCO How too theatrical!

ENRIQUE *suddenly stumbles and falls to the floor with an almighty crash. The food splashes everywhere, and even catches some of the guests.* ENRIQUE *rises with great dignity, bows politely and leaves.*
LUCÍA *breaks the tension. Everyone in the room is shaken by this laughter. The atmosphere is uneasy.*

RUSSELL   It was a joke?

RAÚL   It was on purpose?

LUCÍA   My dear friends, that was planned! Tonight's entertainment has begun!

SILVIA   Divine.

FRANCISCO Oh, *mais . . . c'est exquis*!

RAÚL   Is it possible?

NOBILE   With my wife everything is possible.

ROC   Completely unexpected.

BLANCA   Lucía has her own special 'chic'. Not everyone can make a joke like that in good taste.

RUSSELL   I didn't find it in good taste at all.

RUSSELL *gets up from the table. The other* GUESTS *talk amongst themselves.* LUCÍA *is rather upset.*
A BEAR *can be heard in the distance.* JULIO *comes in accompanied by a bear handler who has a performing bear on a leash for the second part of* LUCÍA's *entertainment.* LUCÍA *gets up and quickly takes* JULIO *to one side.*

9

LUCÍA	I'm just in time! Don't set him free, Julio! Señor Russell doesn't like jokes. Take him to the garden.
JULIO	What about the lambs, Madam?
LUCÍA	Take them to the garden, too.
JULIO	I am relieved Madam has taken this step. There are grave matters which require your urgent attention.
LUCÍA	What matters?
JULIO	Strange things are happening.

PABLO *suddenly appears, putting his coat on.*

LUCÍA	Pablo! Where are you going?
PABLO	Madam . . . I have to see . . . my sister.
LUCÍA	What's the matter with her?
PABLO	The poor girl . . . She took ill this morning . . . and by now . . . I'm afraid . . . she . . .
LUCÍA	Unbelievable! How dare you insult me by leaving now, when all my guests are seated for dinner.
PABLO	Madame, forgive me, but everything is ready to be served.

ENRIQUE *and the last few* SERVANTS *appear, putting their coats on – they freeze when they see* LUCÍA.

LUCÍA	Enrique! All of you. What is your excuse?
ENRIQUE	We're going to see his sister, too.

LUCÍA   It's a conspiracy. This has been planned!

JULIO   Every day the staff grows more impertinent.

ENRIQUE, PABLO, SERVANTS
Forgive us, Marquesa. We'll be back first thing
tomorrow morning.

LUCÍA   On the contrary: if you leave now consider
yourselves fired! Julio! Keep serving on your own!
I am depending on you.

SCENE 6

DRAWING ROOM
*BLANCA is playing the piano. The GUESTS gather around. Back in
the dining room, LETICIA throws an ashtray through a window.
The sound of shattering glass. RAÚL and the COLONEL are
startled.*

RUSSELL   What was that?

COLONEL   An anarchist!

RAÚL   No: it was Leticia, our Valkyrie.

LETICIA enters.

LETICIA   *Con lagrimas la lavaba,*
Con suspiros la espandia.

LEONORA   Oh, what a captivating woman!

EDUARDO and BEATRIZ are dancing slowly together.

EDUARDO   What's your name?

BEATRIZ   Beatriz, and yours?

EDUARDO	Eduardo.
BEATRIZ	Age?
EDUARDO	Thirty years old.
BEATRIZ	Profession?
EDUARDO	Architect.
BEATRIZ	Are you single?
EDUARDO	Till Saturday. Just like you!
BEATRIZ	Just five more days until our wedding!

JULIO pushes the drinks trolley amongst the guests.

LEONORA	Tonight I feel marvellous, Doctor. I've eaten well. There's no doubt: your treatment has transformed me.
DOCTOR	No. There was no gravity in your illness.
LEONORA	What stirring music! So full of nostalgia. Do you dance, Doctor?
DOCTOR	I've never even tried.
LEONORA	How sad! I long only for you to take me in your arms!
DOCTOR	I'm flattered that my patient is so pleased with me but –

LEONORA interrupts and plants a long kiss on his lips. The *DOCTOR* pulls away gasping and escapes.

Transference!

LEONORA   I've been wanting to do that for so long.

FRANCISCO *is agitated.*

SILVIA   Francisco! Did you bring your pills?

FRANCISCO Don't nanny me!

DOCTOR   Is he alright?

SILVIA (*to* FRANCISCO)
           Do you have to eat so much?
       (*to the* DOCTOR)
           His ulcerations have no mercy.

FRANCISCO Sister!

LEONORA   Doctor! Aren't you going to come and listen
           to Blanca?

DOCTOR   In just a moment.

As LEONORA *goes to listen to* BLANCA *play the piano, she opens
her handbag to remove a handkerchief. Two large chicken feet
with feathers can clearly be seen.
The* DOCTOR *and* RAÚL *hold back.*

RAÚL   Why did she kiss you so passionately?

DOCTOR   Poor Leonora! When Transference Neurosis
           develops, a patient's relationship with the doctor
           becomes the most important in her life.

RAÚL   How is her illness progressing? Is there hope?

DOCTOR   None at all. In just three months she'll be
           completely bald.

RAÚL   Lucky for her she has a good skull.

13

They move towards BLANCA, *who is now playing the piano
with extraordinary brilliance.
After a particularly difficult passage* BLANCA *stops playing.
Everyone applauds lightly.*

ALL   Brava, Blanca!

COLONEL Sublime!

NOBILE   Thank you, Blanca.

RAÚL   Magnificent!

ROC   Beautiful, my dear, as always.

LUCÍA   An exquisite interpretation.

RUSSELL   Marvellous!

SILVIA, FRANCISCO
     A delicious performance!

BEATRIZ, EDUARDO, RUSSELL
     What hypnotic playing!

SILVIA, LEONORA, FRANCISCO
     Was it Paradisi?

BLANCA   Yes, it was Paradisi.

LUCÍA, EDUARDO, ROC
     Paradisi!

NOBILE   I wish we had a harpsichord. It would have sounded
     perfect on a harpsichord.

COLONEL (*to* ROC)
     Maestro, what is your opinion of the 'pizzicato' we
     have just heard?

ROC	Not 'pizzicato'! Sonata, Colonel, sonata.
RAÚL	Blanca, something by Adès, I implore you!
BLANCA	You must forgive me. It's very late and I am tired.
NOBILE	Late? This is the loveliest hour, the most intimate part of the evening. Leticia, sing!
ALL	Leticia, you must sing!
RAÚL	I will not leave this house until she sings!
ALL	We will not leave this house until she sings!
ROC	Hasn't the poor thing already sung enough for one night?

ROC *lies down on the sofa. A number of the* GUESTS *prepare to go.*

BLANCA	Lucía, Edmundo. We ought to be going.

SILVIA (*to* LUCÍA)
Let's see each other soon, my dear.

JULIO *is in the dining room.* NOBILE *addresses him from the drawing room without crossing the threshold.*

NOBILE	Julio, will you see to the coats?
JULIO	Yes, sir.

ROC *has fallen asleep.*

NOBILE	Señor Roc! (*trying to rouse* ROC) Is he asleep?
BLANCA	You must forgive him. He felt young tonight and might have drunk a little too much wine.

NOBILE	The Maestro's stamina's quite remarkable – to perform for two hours with such great concentration!
BLANCA	Believe me, he has no trouble performing, even after the opera. He keeps me up all night!
NOBILE	He'd better sleep it off or he might try something here!
BLANCA	Edmundo! He would never dare in front of all these people!
NOBILE	Of course not. I don't know what came over me.

A spell seems to have been cast. LEONORA *has fallen asleep. The* GUESTS *are unaware that they are somehow going around in circles.*

LUCÍA	Silvia! I thought you'd already left.
SILVIA	I just thought I'd pause here a moment.
FRANCISCO	Raúl was explaining how the fauna in Romania . . .
RAÚL	Because the climate is so harsh . . .
SILVIA	But I can't stay here and chat all night! Francisco! Now I'm really going! Where's my wrap?
LUCÍA	I'll find it.

LUCÍA *crosses the room and passes by the* COLONEL*. He follows her discreetly.*
At this moment we are aware that no one in the room is actually leaving. Some are chatting and a number are now seated or lying down.

CLOAKROOM

The COLONEL *pulls* LUCÍA *close and kisses her passionately.*

COLONEL   Why is nobody leaving? It's almost four in the
           morning!

LUCÍA   They'll go very soon. Take advantage of the
           confusion, and wait for me in my bedroom.

COLONEL   But what about your husband?

LUCÍA   If he appears I'll tell him I wanted to show you
           my incunabulum.

They kiss again.

SCENE 8

DRAWING ROOM

Most of the GUESTS *have now sat down, the others are looking
for a seat but there is now only space on the floor. Some of
the men unbutton their collars and loosen their ties. They are
confused, exhausted. A few have fallen asleep.* NOBILE *looks
worried.* LUCÍA *has joined him.*

NOBILE   That went well, despite...

He notices that LUCÍA*'s lips are smudged from the* COLONEL*'s kiss.*

           It must be very late: your lipstick has faded.

He rubs the corner of her mouth with his finger.

           We must attend to our guests and make them
           comfortable.

He switches off some of the lights.

But I love the spontaneity of this. Just like the old days!
(*to the* GUESTS) If you wish to stay the night, we will have rooms prepared. I'm delighted to see the spirit of improvisation is still alive.

COLONEL You are the perfect host, Edmundo, but we must not take advantage of your hospitality.

LETICIA I have a matinee tomorrow afternoon.

RUSSELL And I have a meeting in just four hours' time.

Still no one leaves. Some of the GUESTS *rise to their feet, struggling to stay alert.* JULIO *is across the threshold in the dining room; everyone else is in the drawing room. Someone switches off more lights.*

DOCTOR They're serious. They're turning off the lights.

RUSSELL This is decision time. We must leave at once. If the others are drunk or have gone mad, they can stay.

FRANCISCO *is on the couch with his sister,* SILVIA, *who is stretched out, fast asleep.* RAÚL *removes his tails, waistcoat, collar and tie.*

COLONEL I don't believe this! If it weren't for my great respect for our hosts I'd teach that slob a lesson!

FRANCISCO, RAÚL
These clothes are fit for statues, not men – especially at five in the morning.

FRANCISCO *also removes his tails, waistcoat and tie before stretching out on the couch with* SILVIA. RAÚL *lies down on the floor.*

LUCÍA (*to* NOBILE)
Don't you think they're going a bit far taking off
their tailcoats?

NOBILE   Remember Raúl lives in the United States. They
have different standards. And besides, the body has
its limits, and our house is so well heated.

He removes his tails. LUCÍA *is confounded.*

LUCÍA   But the shame of it!

NOBILE   Precisely why we must stoop to their level.

The clock strikes five. The room is now dark. All of the GUESTS
lie exhausted. JULIO *falls asleep at the empty table across the
threshold in the dining room. An unstoppable force has taken
over . . .*
EDUARDO *and* BEATRIZ *stir. They move to a private corner. They
caress each other sensuously.*

EDUARDO   Our first night together, darling Beatriz.

BEATRIZ   But why are we still here, Eduardo? Why haven't
we gone home?

EDUARDO   Because everybody decided to stay.

BEATRIZ   But is any of this normal?

EDUARDO   Life is funny. And strange. Only the Chinese do not
fear the ghosts that rise from our pores every midnight.

BEATRIZ   I can hardly stand.

EDUARDO   Come here. Let's sleep.

INTERLUDE

19

ACT 2

SCENE 1

DRAWING ROOM
Dawn. Some of the GUESTS *have awakened, others not.* LUCÍA
gets up and crosses to her husband, who is putting on his tails.

NOBILE   What the hell is happening?

LUCÍA   We'll give them breakfast. Then they're bound
              to leave.

NOBILE   I hope so. I trust you. Look, Lucía! There's
              something wrong with Señor Russell.

NOBILE and LUCÍA *go to him quickly.*
BLANCA, LEONORA *and* SILVIA *are now awake.*

BLANCA   How did you sleep, Leonora?

LEONORA   All through the night!

SILVIA   But I, oh God! What a night! I slept worse than
              I did on that night-train to Nice that derailed
              and crashed.

LEONORA   You were in that train crash? How exciting!

SILVIA   I ran from one end of the train to the other like
              a madwoman. A third-class carriage was crushed
              like a giant concertina. It was carnage. I must be
              insensitive because the pain of those poor, common
              people didn't affect me at all.

LETICIA   I'm hungry. Has no one in this house heard of
              breakfast?

SILVIA   I'm going to arrange myself. I must look dreadful.
               You all look dreadful. Isn't this fun!

SILVIA straightens FRANCISCO*'s hair with her fingers. He pushes
her away brusquely.*
RUSSELL *is stretched out on a sofa. He breathes laboriously. The*
DOCTOR *has been examining him.*

LETICIA   He had a very rough night. I heard him struggling
               for breath. Then he lost consciousness.

LEONORA   He did seem strange last night. What do you think,
               Doctor?

DOCTOR   In a few hours he'll be completely bald.

LEONORA   What does that mean?

DOCTOR   He has only hours to live.

LEONORA   How horrible! And you're never wrong! I don't feel
               very well myself.

She goes to kiss his hand. He pulls away firmly.

DOCTOR   Nonsense.

LUCÍA *looks at* JULIO, *who is just beyond the threshold, in the
dining room.*

LUCÍA   Julio, please do your best to provide breakfast
               for our guests.

JULIO   I'm sorry, Madame, but no delivery men have come.

LUCÍA   Not even the milkman?

JULIO   No, which is odd.

LUCÍA   There's still cold food left over from last night.
             Bring that and coffee.

LETICIA, SILVIA, BLANCA
             Lucía, my dear, excuse me but is there a place
             we can go to arrange ourselves?

LUCÍA   Of course! At once! Let's go to my boudoir.

LETICIA, SILVIA, BLANCA
             Let's go to her boudoir.

LEONORA *lies on the sofa, now suddenly much weaker.* EDUARDO,
the COLONEL *and* RAÚL *are now observing the ladies as they cross
the room.*

COLONEL   Gentlemen, quickly! Watch the ladies. I'll bet you
             anything that they do not leave this room.

As the LADIES *approach the threshold they turn to each other
and hover. Without realising it, they wander from the exit and
begin to mingle with the other guests. Another failed exit.*

             You see? I told you! What can it mean?

RAÚL   I don't know. There is no explanation.

COLONEL   Last night, after the party, none of us made the
             slightest attempt to go home. Spending all night
             in this room, ignoring the most elementary
             conventions and turning it into an infernal gypsy
             camp.

LEONORA, RUSSELL
             Go home.

SILVIA   I find it highly original. I adore anything that
             deviates from the norm.

22

LETICIA	Yes, we've all noticed that, Silvia. I don't like this one bit, but I didn't say anything because I am too polite.
RAÚL	Come now. Don't exaggerate. We were under the spell of the music, enchanted by the talk. What's so strange about that?
DOCTOR	Perhaps our friend Lucía could explain why she had breakfast served in here, instead of in the dining room?
LUCÍA	Well, I don't know, Doctor . . . Since we were all in this room already, I thought . . .
RAÚL	The Doctor loves to play Sherlock Holmes.
BLANCA	I must go home. The children will be distraught. Alberto!
BLANCA, ROC	
	We're leaving now.
ROC	This is completely absurd.
BLANCA	Silvia!
BLANCA, ROC	
	Vamos!

ROC *and* BLANCA *walk off. As they move towards the doorway, their resolve weakens.*

SILVIA	No! Not yet. What are we going to do on the streets at this hour of the morning?
BLANCA	Silvia, in the name of God! You are a mother, too. You have a little boy who has to go to school!

SILVIA   But my son has a private tutor at home! El Padre
            Sansón. Very cultured and wise, with the most
            exquisite manners. My late husband used to say
            he had all the features of a saint.

FRANCISCO   What nonsense! Your husband didn't trust him
            around the boy. He was no fool!

ROC   Don Francisco! Duchess! This is no time to
            confabulate about priests.

ALL   *Vamos!*

*A final, desperate, push to escape is suddenly scuppered by the
arrival of the breakfast trolley.*

JULIO   Ladies and gentlemen, breakfast is served.

LETICIA   No! Julio! Don't cross over!

*Everyone waits, torn between the danger JULIO is in and their
hunger for breakfast. ROC stares at the steaming coffee.*

COLONEL, ROC
            What harm can a cup of coffee do?

ROC   And I can't smoke on an empty stomach.

LUCÍA looks to her husband for guidance. He nods.

LUCÍA   Of course! Julio, please come through. Would you
            care to join us, Blanca?

*BLANCA falls despairingly into a chair. JULIO serves coffee. Some
of the GUESTS form a queue.*

RAÚL   Why this ominous mood? Why are we creating this
            atmosphere of catastrophe? It's not the first time
            I've found myself at a party at eight in the morning.

24

JULIO serves the cold meats and coffee. LETICIA calmly eats but most of the other GUESTS ignore the food. An atmosphere of sadness descends on the room. FRANCISCO searches in vain for a coffee spoon.

FRANCISCO Forgive me, Lucía, but there are no coffee spoons. These spoons are teaspoons. These spoons are too large. I can't stir my coffee with a teaspoon.

LUCÍA Forgive me, Francisco, but Julio is all on his own. Julio, please go back to the kitchen and bring us some coffee spoons.

JULIO Yes, madam.

He walks towards the door but stops before crossing the threshold. Nearby the DOCTOR and the COLONEL observe his indecision.

But first – would any of the gentlemen like something to eat? Ladies? Cold meats? Viennoiseries?

COLONEL Nothing, Julio! Go where you've been told!

JULIO is confused.

JULIO Wouldn't it be more prudent if I wait until everyone has finished?

LUCÍA What's going on, Julio? Did you not hear me? I asked you to bring us the spoons. Now go!

JULIO does his best to cross back over the threshold but now cannot do it.

LUCÍA What's wrong with you, Julio? Are you ill?

JULIO cannot speak. BLANCA *is now crying helplessly.* LUCÍA *goes to her.*

Blanca! Why are you crying?

COLONEL   What is the Doctor's opinion?

DOCTOR   The butler's strange resistance against obeying orders confirms my observations. Since last night, not one of us, try as he might, has been able to leave this room. What is happening to us?

Fear is in the air. A huge thunderstorm outside. Thunder cracks, lightning flashes. The room slowly moves into shadow. Time passes. It is evening. Confidence has given way to despondency. Everyone is silent. BLANCA *plays the piano. At the end we hear the clock strike seven.*

PIANO INTERLUDE

BLANCA   Over the sea,
over the sea,
Where is the way?
Birds, tell me!

Over the sea
on islands of gold
a mighty tall nation
of giants stroll.

A mighty tall nation
upright and pure,
ruled by a king
like none before.

Gardens the king has
over the sea
where birds of paradise
nest in the trees.

Over the sea,
over the sea,
where is the way?
Birds, tell me!

BLANCA *stares at the keyboard.* LETICIA *suddenly bangs the piano lid down forcefully, just missing* BLANCA's *hands.*

LETICIA   There is a seriously ill man in the room!

The DOCTOR *is now examining* RUSSELL, *who is unconscious.*

COLONEL   What is the Doctor's opinion?

DOCTOR   I see no need to hide the truth. He has fallen into
            a coma and I have no medicine! Please! You must
            help me take Señor Russell to where he can get
            medical help.

Everyone is listless, weak.

COLONEL   Dr Conde is right! This inertia must stop. Who will
            take this man out of the house?

RAÚL   Why don't you do it? We will all be right behind
            you!

FRANCISCO We are lost! Silvia! Why did you bring me here?

SILVIA   Francisco, please calm down. I am not to blame!
            Don't blame me!

BEATRIZ   There is no water left! Coffee! I'm dying of thirst. Julio!

JULIO   Señorita, I'm sorry, there's not a drop left!

EDUARDO *throws some flowers from a vase and offers the stinking water.*

EDUARDO   The flower water smells a bit, but a squeeze of lemon will take away the taste.

He picks up a lemon from the floor and squeezes it into the water.

BEATRIZ   Eurgh! No thank you, Eduardo. I'd rather wait.

LETICIA   I am going to smash another window.

RAÚL   What for? There is a door! I don't understand. There must be an explanation. Are we going mad?

BLANCA   We've been here twenty-four hours and no one has come for us. We've been completely forgotten.

ROC   I don't understand the people out there. They should have done something by now!

COLONEL   Unless they're all dead and we are the only survivors.

LEONORA   Why don't they come to save us?

ROC   This all began with the desertion of the servants. What reason did they give?

NOBILE   Please, Roc, there's no reason to form alarmist theories.

RAÚL   The same reason rats desert a sinking ship.

NOBILE   I am sure they had very good reason to leave.

JULIO   No sir, they had no reason.

RAÚL, ROC   So there is no reason!

The DOCTOR *has become hysterical.*

DOCTOR   We must remain completely calm. This can't go on
            for ever. That is scientifically impossible. We are
            not 'enchanted'. This is no magician's house. Only
            by clinical analysis can we conquer our abulia.

LETICIA, SILVIA, BEATRIZ, BLANCA, LEONORA, FRANCISCO,
EDUARDO, RAÚL, COLONEL, ROC
            Abulia?

*Several people have been trying to escape. Everyone is extremely
agitated. Some try, but fail, to leave.*

NOBILE   Silence! I have an idea. Let's all join in a last
            supreme effort of will to get out of this room.

RAÚL   Silence. You're to blame! You led us into this trap!
            We are the victims of this twisted joke because
            of you.

NOBILE   Because of me? Because I invited you to dine?

RAÚL   You invited us to your house (*sarcastically*) 'to dine
            with you after the opera'. I could have gone to
            bed. Or to the brothel. Anywhere but here! Why
            this strange invitation?

NOBILE   Strange? You all said you were 'delighted'. Even
            you, Raúl.

RAÚL   Well, I've changed my mind.

29

NOBILE   I think you're losing your mind!

LETICIA   Edmundo is right, Raúl. You are an idiot.

RAÚL is livid. He stares threateningly into LETICIA's face.

RAÚL   If you weren't a woman . . .

LETICIA suddenly slaps RAÚL. And then a second time.

FRANCISCO What are the men doing to solve this impasse? They are blabbing and blabbing like a lot of girls.

RUSSELL is breathing laboriously.

SILVIA   Calm down, Francisco. Remember your ulcerations.

FRANCISCO Silvia, find a way out of here.

SILVIA   My brother suffers from anxiety.

FRANCISCO I will never set foot in this hideous house again!

FRANCISCO bursts into tears.

SILVIA   It is his nerves. This is affecting him more than everyone else.

LUCÍA, BLANCA, LEONORA, NOBILE, COLONEL, DOCTOR
     Calm down, Francisco.

The DOCTOR takes RUSSELL's pulse. RUSSELL stirs and gives the DOCTOR a dazed look.

SILVIA   He's so sensitive – like a little girl.

FRANCISCO Shut up! All of you. You're making it worse! Leave me alone!

RUSSELL forces a grimace that wants to be a smile.

RUSSELL   I am happy . . . so happy . . . I won't see the
              Extermination.

RUSSELL *collapses back into a coma. The* DOCTOR *is astonished.*
EDUARDO *and* BEATRIZ *have been watching* RUSSELL *and the*
DOCTOR.
LETICIA *is hovering with* SILVIA *around a walk-in cabinet*
which is being used as a lavatory. SILVIA *knocks on the door in*
desperation. It opens slowly. BLANCA *comes out.* SILVIA *goes in.*
Some of the others begin to fall asleep.

BEATRIZ   I don't mind dying, but not like this – surrounded
              by people like this. I want to die alone with you,
              Eduardo.

EDUARDO   That is my greatest fear. That we can never be
              alone.

BEATRIZ   There is one way we can be alone.

EDUARDO   How, Beatriz?

BEATRIZ   Follow me when they fall asleep.

SILVIA *comes out of the walk-in cabinet.* LETICIA *goes in.*

BLANCA, SILVIA
              When I lifted the lid,
              I saw a huge precipice,
              and a river rushing far below.
              And as I sat down,
              an eagle flew by forty feet below.

LETICIA *comes out of the walk-in cabinet.*

LETICIA   And as I stood up, the wind blew a gust of dead
              leaves in my face.

The clock strikes two. The DOCTOR *looks sadly at* RUSSELL, *who has now died, and places his handkerchief over the old man's face. He tiptoes over to the* COLONEL *who is lying down.*

DOCTOR   Consummatum est!

COLONEL   That's the last thing we need.

DOCTOR   When they see him they'll despair.

COLONEL   If only our bodies would evaporate when we die.

DOCTOR   What shall we do with it?

The two men straighten up the body of RUSSELL, *and pick it up.*

COLONEL   Señor Roc should have died instead. What's one
                      conductor more or less in the world?

EDUARDO *and* BEATRIZ *lie together, hidden.*

EDUARDO   This is where the ocean ends.

BEATRIZ   It's too far for me to reach.

EDUARDO   Just go a little further down.

BEATRIZ, EDUARDO
                      Into the fold . . .
                      Yes, there it is!
                      The rictus!
                      It's horrible!
                      My love! My refuge! My death!

During this the DOCTOR *and the* COLONEL *slowly drag* RUSSELL's
dead body across the room and into the walk-in cabinet.

INTERVAL

ACT 3

OUTSIDE THE HOUSE
POLICEMEN *wander around, guarding the house. The sound of a* CROWD *can be heard but not seen.*

CHORUS 1   What can we do?
            Nothing!

CHORUS 2   What can we do? This can't last for ever. We want
            to go in. Why do we not? There's nothing to stop
            us. Send in the army!

CHORUS 1   No! They already did. Fully equipped. But not one
            man entered the house.

CHORUS 2   But did they try?

CHORUS 1 and 2
            No! That's what's so serious.

Some of the CROWD *have appeared and stumble towards the gates of the house. The* POLICE *struggle to stop them.*

POLICE   Stand back!

CHORUS (*offstage*)
            Let us in!

POLICE   Don't push!

CHORUS   We want to see!

POLICE   Stay where you are!

CHORUS   They must be freed!

33

The CROWD *has grown in size. A scuffle.*

POLICE   Keep out!

CHORUS   Let us pass!

POLICE   Get back!

CHORUS   They need our help!

POLICE   You're not allowed!

CHORUS   We'll get them out!

POLICE   You have been warned!

Some POLICEMEN *draw guns.*

CHORUS   Don't shoot!

POLICE   Don't move!

CHORUS   We're not dogs!

POLICE   Not one more step!

CHORUS   We're going in!

POLICE   You have to stop!

CHORUS   Down with the pigs!

POLICE   You must go back!

The CROWD *finally overwhelms and surges past the* POLICEMEN, *and then, just as suddenly, they stop, helpless.*

DRAWING ROOM

JULIO is hacking into a part of the drawing room wall with a ceremonial axe. The GUESTS anxiously stand around staring at him. They are now smeared with dirt, their clothes half-shredded. LEONORA and ROC are too ill to take part. JULIO has now revealed a water pipe deep in the wall. RAÚL rushes over with a second axe and joins him for a final push. Suddenly an enormous gush of water bursts forth.

ALL   Water!

They all rush forward, pushing and jostling.

RAÚL   It's so cold!

FRANCISCO Let me through!

COLONEL (*to FRANCISCO*)
            Ladies first!

ALL   I'm dying of thirst!

LETICIA, SILVIA, BLANCA
            My hands have shrivelled up like dead roots!

BLANCA takes water to ROC.

DOCTOR   Drink, my dear friends. One at a time! Get in
            a line! Just one cup each, please! Too much at once
            could be dangerous, especially for the sick.

LETICIA is next to LEONORA, who looks dreadful. LEONORA has a fever but no water to drink. No one seems to care.

LEONORA   I'm dying of thirst.

FRANCISCO I've got a temperature!

People collide and struggle as they hold out old cups and glasses towards the clear, cold water. FRANCISCO *pushes through to the front. The* COLONEL *pulls him away.*

COLONEL   Can't you hear? Ladies first!

SILVIA *runs to her brother.*

SILVIA   Colonel, you're a dictator. I will not let you
          brutalise my brother.

SILVIA *offers* FRANCISCO *her water.*

BLANCA   I wish we'd never found water. It only prolongs
          the agony.

SILVIA   Then don't drink any!

OBSESSIVE COMPULSIVE BALLET

SILVIA *and* LUCÍA *wash in the pool of water,* BLANCA *combs her hair,* LETICIA *squeezes a spot,* FRANCISCO *shaves his leg,* NOBILE *tears strips off his shirt, and* RAÚL *and the* COLONEL *pluck at their nose hairs.* JULIO *tears pieces of paper, rolling them into balls, chewing some. The* DOCTOR *watches sadly as they repeat these actions over and over.*

BLANCA   I am so hungry! Julio, isn't there just one sugar
          cube left?

LEONORA, ROC
          We are so hungry, Julio! Isn't there just one sugar
          cube left?

36

JULIO   I am so sorry, Madame. There's been nothing for
         days. The delivery men have not been.

BLANCA, ROC
         What are you eating, Julio? Isn't there just one
         sugar cube left?

JULIO   It is paper, Madame. It tastes better than it looks.
         It is made from the tender bark of young trees.
         It can't hurt. Would you like a piece?

FRANCISCO I can't stand it any more. The way that bitch combs
         half her hair! I would rather starve or die of thirst
         than look at her!

SILVIA pulls the comb from BLANCA's hands.

SILVIA   Why don't you comb your hair properly? Like this!
         Down! All the way down!

*She drags the comb through the back of BLANCA's hair like a
maniac.*

BLANCA   Ow!

*SILVIA snaps the comb in pieces and storms off. BLANCA bursts
into tears.*

FRANCISCO I hate her!

He searches frantically in his pockets.

         Excuse me, Lucia, but have you seen a small silver
         box with white pills inside?

LUCÍA   A box? No! I'm sorry.

SILVIA   It's the medication for my brother's ulcerations.

LUCÍA   I'll look for it.

SILVIA   You must be patient, my love. We'll find it!

FRANCISCO   Someone's hidden it so my ulcers burst and I die!

SILVIA   Please don't talk like that, my darling!

FRANCISCO *and* SILVIA *hug and caress each other a little too
closely for a brother and sister.*
RAÚL *is watching.*

FRANCISCO   What are you looking at?

RAÚL   What do I care if you are in love with your sister,
            you incestuous little man?

FRANCISCO   Filthy pig! I have known all along that your mind
            was depraved.

RAÚL   Deviant!

NOBILE   Gentlemen, please, behave! We are all in the same
            situation.

SILVIA, FRANCISCO, RAÚL
            You old hypocrite, Nobile, lecturing us when all this
            is your fault!

NOBILE   All my fault? Why? I who hate suffering, and have
            devoted my life to preventing it? How could you
            think that I . . .

COLONEL   Ignore them, Nobile.

LUCÍA *joins the* COLONEL, *not her husband.*

LUCÍA   Álvaro, I'm so hungry! You must think of a way
            to get out of here!

38

The COLONEL *takes her hand.*

COLONEL   We'd need a miracle!

LUCÍA   Edmundo and I have sworn to celebrate a Solemn
High Requiem if we are delivered from this hell.

The COLONEL *draws* LUCÍA*'s head close to him and kisses her on
the cheek.* NOBILE *turns away confused.* LUCÍA *breathes in the air
with an expression of disgust. She wretches.*

This unbearable stench!

Part of the stench is RUSSELL*'s body. Someone is trying to keep
the door of the walk-in cabinet shut with a chair. Another tries
to tape over the cracks.*

COLONEL   We're trying to contain it.

BLANCA *(pulling small tufts out of her hair)*
Where are my children now? What are they doing?

DOCTOR   Blanca! Your hair. Remember what I told you!

SILVIA   My poor son, Yoli! I hope Padre Sansón is taking
care of him!

LEONORA   I'm cold! I can't bear it any more, Doctor. I want
to die. Can't you kill me and end this pain?

DOCTOR   Don't talk like that! Your pain comes and goes,
and soon will disappear completely.

The DOCTOR *goes to leave.*

LEONORA   Don't leave me, Doctor! Your presence comforts
me. If we escape and I am cured, will you take me
to Lourdes? Promise me!

DOCTOR   I promise.

LEONORA   We will prostrate ourselves at the feet of the Virgin,
          for only she will get us out of here.

DOCTOR   Stop! You must rest.

LEONORA   When we go to Lourdes I want you to buy me
          a washable rubber Virgin. Promise me!

LETICIA   I'm hungry.

LEONORA   I'm cold.

DOCTOR   We need painkillers more than food. But we have
          neither.

BLANCA joins FRANCISCO. *He glances at her out of the corner
of his eye. He is repulsed.*

FRANCISCO *Vous sentez la hyène.*

BLANCA   What did you say?

FRANCISCO You smell like a hyena.

BLANCA   How dare you insult me!

COLONEL   Shame on you.

FRANCISCO Why are you afraid of the truth? She stinks! And so
           do you. And so do I. We all stink! And Russell's
           corpse stinks worst of all! We are pigs! This is a
           pigsty! You're all disgusting!
           I hate you! I hate you! I hate you! I hate you!
           And you, and you, and you, and you, and you, and
           you, and you, and you, and you, and you, and . . .

SILVIA   Francisco!

40

NOBILE   Here it is. Barbarity, violence, filth. Everything
           I've hated most since childhood. Our inseparable
           companions. Death is preferable to this degradation.

INTERLUDE

Evening approaches. Everything is ghostly; the noise of machine-
gun fire in the distance. Bodies are scattered everywhere, some
living, some dead.

LEONORA *is now very sick and delirious. As she wanders*
aimlessly a severed hand appears in front of her eyes. She
follows it, panic-stricken, as it floats around the room. At one
point it floats on to LUCÍA's *neck as if to strangle her, but she*
remains asleep. LEONORA *is terrified.*

LEONORA   I think they watch us from time to time
            from the front from the back from the sides
            The rancorous eyes of hens
            more dreadful than the rotting water of grottoes
            Incestuous as the eyes of the mother who died
                on the gallows.
            I think I will have to die with my hands in the
                quagmire . . .
            I think that if a son were born to me
            he would remain eternally watching the beasts
                copulating in the late afternoon!

In her hallucination she tries to stop the hand but fails to make
any impact as it dissolves in space before reappearing again
across the room. It now moves towards BLANCA *who is slumped*
over a small table asleep. As it slides across the table towards
BLANCA's *neck* LEONORA *grabs a dagger and prepares to attack,*

41

but BLANCA's *real hand has now replaced the floating hand.*
LEONORA *lifts the dagger high in the air and stabs it down
into* BLANCA's *hand.* BLANCA *screams out in pain.*

BLANCA   My hand!

DOCTOR   Leonora! What have you done?

RAÚL   Tie her up.

LETICIA   Get her out of here now!

RAÚL   Call an ambulance!

BLANCA *is sobbing.*

DOCTOR   She has a high fever. We must bring it down.

They lay a damp cloth on her forehead.

SILVIA (*to* BLANCA)
           Don't cry. It's over. We'll watch her. She won't do it
           again.

SCENE 3

EDUARDO *and* BEATRIZ *lie together inside a walk-in cabinet.*

EDUARDO   What is today?

BEATRIZ   Why?

EDUARDO   How long have we been in this room? A month?
           More?

BEATRIZ   No, not so long. We would have died by now
           without food.

BEATRIZ, EDUARDO
   I feel as if I'd always been here. I feel as if we'll
   always be here. Unless?

EDUARDO   Unless we escape together.

BEATRIZ, EDUARDO
   Lose ourselves in the shadows.

BEATRIZ   Wherever you go, I'll follow you, Eduardo.

EDUARDO   My darling little corpse.

He smiles.

BEATRIZ, EDUARDO
   Fold your body into mine,
   Hide yourself within its hand.
   Flayed, you showed me muscles of wood,
   bouquets of lust I'll make from your veins.

   What longing, what desires of shattered seas
   Changed to nickel
   Will be born, birds of our coupled mouths,
   While death enters through our feet.

SCENE 4

*Everyone is scattered around, asleep. In the shadows ROC glides
into the air and flies across the room like a winged vampire.
He descends ominously and lowers himself on top of LETICIA's
sleeping body, where he attempts to molest her. LETICIA wakes
suddenly and screams.*

LETICIA   Aagh! Don't touch me! What are you doing?

43

ROC *flies away into the darkness.*

NOBILE   What was that?

RAÚL   It was the Colonel!

NOBILE   What was the Colonel?

RAÚL (*to the* COLONEL)
          I am not blind, sir!
      (*to* NOBILE)
          The Colonel's an incubus, not a gentleman.

COLONEL   You dog, Yebenes!

DOCTOR   Gentlemen! Don't demean yourselves.

RAÚL   He sneaks around in the dark like a thief.

NOBILE   What happened?

RAÚL   This man tried to rape Leticia.

COLONEL   What? You filthy . . .

DOCTOR   Enough! This is beneath you all. Remember who
          you are!

LEONORA *lies exhausted.*

LEONORA   Please, have mercy!

NOBILE   Allow me to make a suggestion for everyone's sake.
          If the ladies sleep on one side of the room and men
          on the other –

COLONEL   Marquis! You're speaking to gentlemen, not rapists.

NOBILE   I only meant it is in everyone's interest . . .

RAÚL (*to* NOBILE)
Ignore the Colonel, he's a pervert!

LUCÍA   Edmundo stop! You're making a fool of yourself!

LETICIA   Edmundo is right, Lucía!

BLANCA   Why can't they stop fighting and find us some food.

DOCTOR   Stop! Don't you understand? Can't you see?

Out of nowhere a number of large LAMBS *appear across
the threshold in the dining room. Everyone is bewildered,
dumbstruck. The* LAMBS *walk fearlessly towards the drawing
room.*
The GUESTS *part like the Red Sea as the* LAMBS *come into the
room.* JULIO *picks up a ceremonial axe and raises it in the air to
kill one of them . . .*
*Suddenly a great looming shadow moves across the back wall
of the adjoining room. The* GUESTS *turn to see the* BEAR. *Three
terrifying roars.*
Blackout. Bang offstage.

SCENE 5

OUTSIDE THE HOUSE
POLICEMEN *and the* ARMY *hover with guns.*
MENI, CAMILA, LUCAS, ENRIQUE *and* PABLO *stand by the gates.*

CHORUS   Quiet as a tomb. The house is in quarantine.

LUCAS   They say that contaminated air sometimes blows
          out to the street.

45

MENI, CAMILA, ENRIQUE, PABLO, SERVANTS
Maybe the food we left behind in the kitchen
has rotted.

CHORUS   Are they all dead? That is to be hoped.

*PADRE SANSÓN approaches with YOLI. The CROWD drifts along
behind them.*

PADRE SANSÓN
Come along, Yoli! Remember you must be good.

POLICEMEN Who are you? Where d'you think you're going?

PADRE SANSÓN
I'm Padre Sansón. I represent Silvia, Duchess of
Ávila. I brought the Duke to see the house.

PADRE, MENI, CAMILA, ENRIQUE, PABLO, CHORUS
His mother is inside.

MENI, CAMILA
And so are all our things!

LUCAS   Wait! I know what to do. We should send the boy in.

MENI, CAMILA, ENRIQUE, PABLO, CHORUS
Send the boy in.

POLICEMEN He's just a child.

MENI, CAMILA, LUCAS, ENRIQUE, PABLO, CHORUS
But he might get through! Let him in.

*The CROWD jostles YOLI to the front. He begins to walk towards
the house.*

Go on, Yoli!
Keep going, Yoli.

Yes, Yoli.
Keep walking, Yoli.
Don't stop!

YOLI gets closer and closer to the house and then suddenly stops.
He turns to look at the CROWD, *frozen, before running back and*
into PADRE SANSÓN's *arms.*

CHORUS   Ah!
           No!

ENRIQUE   What happened?

PABLO   Why did he stop?

MENI grabs YOLI *and tries to push him forward again.*

MENI   Try again! Try a little harder.

As she forces him forward, YOLI *bites her. She cries out in pain.*

YOLI   Mama!

PADRE SANSÓN
    Why did you stop?

CAMILA   Try! Try!

CHORUS   Let's go.
           It's over.
           Let's go home.

The disappointed CROWD *dwindles away.*

PADRE SANSÓN
    Never trust a child.

They leave.

SCENE 6

DRAWING ROOM
The GUESTS *have been preparing to light a fire.* RAÚL *is hacking into a beautiful cello and various items of furniture with the ceremonial axe. The hides of some sheep lie discarded beside a few well-chewed bones.*
JULIO *takes a hunk of half-raw meat from someone who has been holding it to the flames.*
NOBILE *sits alone. His head is bandaged.* LUCÍA *joins him.*

LUCÍA   Edmundo, darling, how do you feel?

NOBILE   My head.

LUCÍA   Savages! They're all savages! I will never forgive them.

ROC   The lamb is perfectly cooked.

BLANCA   Delicious!

RAÚL (*adding more cello to the fire*)
     A little pink for me.

FRANCISCO   Mine's too tough. I prefer it *à point*.

SILVIA   It needs salt.

DOCTOR   We must maintain standards of hygiene unless we want to descend to the level of animals. I'll arrange a cleaning timetable.

NOBILE   My darling, lamb for you?

LUCÍA   Thank you, my dear.

NOBILE   Bon appétit!

48

LEONORA *remains isolated, weak, delirious.*

LEONORA   I had a premonition. That night, before the opera,
I heard a voice saying: 'The keys! The keys!
Don't forget the keys!'

BLANCA   The keys, Leonora?

LEONORA   In the Kabbalah, all the objects that open the door
to the unknown are called the keys.

LEONORA *opens her handbag and takes out two chicken claws.
She gives one to* BLANCA *and the other to* LETICIA.

Now, Blanca, hold it tight! And you, Leticia,
upside-down!

LEONORA *is fixated on the chicken claws.*

LETICIA   I can't read them!

LETICIA, BLANCA, LEONORA
We need blood. The blood of an innocent.

FRANCISCO *is lying against the walk-in cabinet door. A red liquid
stain slowly appears on his shirt. It grows bigger and bigger.*

SILVIA   Blood!!

FRANCISCO Where?

SILVIA   All over you. Help! Help! My brother's been hurt.

A terrified FRANCISCO *thinks he has been injured but then sees a
small stream of blood leaking out from underneath the cabinet
door. He gets up fearfully and opens it.*

FRANCISCO No! Look! In there!

SILVIA *looks inside and screams.* EDUARDO *and* BEATRIZ *lie in a pool of blood, their suicide pact complete.*

RAÚL   Gruesome!

SILVIA   Eduardo! Beatriz!

COLONEL   How did they do it?

DOCTOR   It makes no difference.

BLANCA   They died in mortal sin.

FRANCISCO *laughs nervously, hysterically.*

RAÚL   What's wrong with you?

FRANCISCO   I was thinking. What would you do if I pushed you
            out of the room?

RAÚL   And what if I were to throw your pathetic box
            of pills out of here? You little queer!

RAÚL *takes* FRANCISCO's *silver pill box from his pocket. He throws it up and out of the room.*

FRANCISCO   No! I'll kill you! Silvia!

FRANCISCO *runs to* SILVIA. *She cradles a lamb's carcass in her arms.*

SILVIA   It's very late now.
            Yoli, it's bedtime.
            Don't you feel sleepy
            When you close your eyes?

            Do not fear that man with the goat beard.
            He's just your guardian angel.

Close all the windows,
Yoli, close your eyes,
Or in their millions
Flies will swarm inside.

I'll tuck you in, child of all my dreams.
I'll never see you again.
Goodnight, my son.

YOLI (*offstage*)
Goodnight, Mama.

Everyone is hypnotised by SILVIA.
A sound in the distance. The GUESTS *freeze, fearful of the
unknown. As they look across the threshold, the* BEAR *lumbers
into the dining room. Everyone is spellbound.*

ENSEMBLE   Look!
Up there!
Don't move!
Stand still!
El Papa!
Look!
How solemn!
Majestic.
A warrior!

CHORUS (*offstage*)
Libera de morte aeterna, et lux aeterna luceat.

LEONORA   If Nobile was dead, all this would end.

SILVIA   When the spider dies, the web unravels.

BLANCA   If he had any decency, he'd know what to do!

SILVIA, LEONORA, FRANCISCO, ROC
> He must die.

SILVIA, BLANCA, LEONORA, FRANCISCO, RAÚL, ROC
> *Cridia estroche eka per crilo.*
> *Idrios celian tankar*
> *Alora e cor per atores*
> *Non plivia credoyar.*

DOCTOR　　Ladies, I command you. Be quiet!

RAÚL and FRANCISCO are deep in conversation.

> And you, gentlemen, what are you plotting?

FRANCISCO, RAÚL
> We must kill him. We must kill Nobile.

DOCTOR　　Kill Nobile? You are insane. This is completely irrational.

LEONORA　　A sacrifice.

FRANCISCO　We don't care if it's irrational. When he is dead all this will end.

ROC　　We have to get out!

DOCTOR　　But consider the terrible consequences. There can be no end to the violence!

COLONEL　　If all they want is a fight, I am happy to oblige!

RAÚL　　Álvaro, get out of the way. We have nothing against you or the Doctor. We have to kill Nobile!

ROC　　There is no choice.

RAÚL, ROC　We have to kill Nobile!

BLANCA   Better late than never!

DOCTOR   Listen to me.

SILVIA   Why is the Doctor trying to stop us?

SILVIA, FRANCISCO
           Kill him too!

DOCTOR   This is the end of all human dignity. You are all
           turning into animals.

RAÚL (*to* DOCTOR *and* COLONEL)
           Out of the way!

ROC   Where has he gone?

BLANCA   He is hiding! He's with the Valkyrie!

LUCÍA   No!

SILVIA, BLANCA, LEONORA, FRANCISCO, RAÚL, ROC
           Kill him!

DOCTOR   You're making it worse, Blanca!

RAÚL   Just stay out of this, Doctor.

COLONEL   That's enough, Raúl!

RAÚL   Get your hands off me!

Suddenly NOBILE *appears.*

NOBILE   Silence.
           I will make the sacrifice.

LETICIA   Wait! Don't move! All of you – stay where you are.
           It's strange. How long have we been here? I've
           forgotten. Think how many times we've changed

53

places during this horrible eternity. But now at this moment all of us are in exactly the same positions we were in that night. Or am I hallucinating again?

COLONEL   It's true. I was standing here, and you –

He looks to LUCÍA.

LUCÍA   Here, next to you. And next to me –

SILVIA   Me. Just as I am now.

LEONORA   And I was here.

BLANCA   And I sat at the piano.

LETICIA   Blanca, what did you play?

BLANCA   Paradisi.

LETICIA   Play it! Just the end, Blanca! Play!

BLANCA *is reticent. Only one of her hands can play. The other is bandaged from the stab wound. She sits at the beaten-up piano. The others slowly remember where they were when* BLANCA *played that night after dinner. The* COLONEL *goes to* ROC *and helps him into position.* LUCÍA *and* NOBILE *half-heartedly act as hosts, reminding people where they were.* BLANCA *plays with one hand, her technique shaky. The* GUESTS *now stand where they were during her Act I recital. She finally reaches the last notes.*

LETICIA   Applaud! Applaud!

SILVIA, LEONORA, FRANCISCO, ROC
         Brava!

LETICIA   Blanca, you stood up.

BLANCA *stands up.*

54

Who spoke first? Try to remember!

SILVIA, LEONORA, FRANCISCO
Was it Paradisi?

BLANCA   Yes! It was Paradisi.

NOBILE   I wish we had a harpsichord. It would have sounded
perfect on a harpsichord.

COLONEL (*to* ROC)
Maestro, what is your opinion of the 'pizzicato'
we have just heard?

ROC   Not 'pizzicato'! Sonata, Colonel, sonata.

RAÚL *is now convinced by* LETICIA. *He steps forward.*

RAÚL   Blanca, something by Adès, I implore you!

BLANCA   You must forgive me. It's very late and I am tired.

NOBILE   Late? This is the loveliest hour, the most intimate
part of the evening.

LUCÍA, SILVIA, BLANCA, LEONORA, FRANCISCO, NOBILE, RAÚL,
COLONEL, DOC, *later* ROC, JULIO
Leticia, you must sing!

LETICIA *looks anxious as they plead. This time she knows she
must sing.*

LETICIA   My home, do you ask of my peace, who ask for yours?
To re-ascend your mountains,
Bedew them with my tears,
Press my face into your earth,
Kiss your soil and your rocks.
I'd leave great Spain for one glimpse of your dust.

55

We, your scattered sheep, prisoners of desire
From the four ends of the earth
Our dreaming spirits yearn.
I am the wail of jackals,
I am the violin for your songs.
My heart is with you, the rest is here.

If I'd eagles' wings, I'd fly to you.
Your air is alive with souls,
Your light not of the sun, nor the moon, nor
    the stars.
Happy we the chosen, who live to see your dawn.
In its light
We are restored.

The GUESTS *weep, pray, steel themselves.* JULIO *offers them fragments of coats and wraps which are accepted gracefully. They stumble towards the threshold and attempt to cross over into the dining room. Miraculously they escape. They are free. Gradually a* CROWD *including* LUCAS, MENI, CAMILA, ENRIQUE, PABLO, PADRE SANSÓN, YOLI *and* POLICEMEN *drift in. At first they are frightened, horrified at the sight of the emaciated, unrecognisable* GUESTS. *People greet each other, overcome with emotion.* YOLI *runs to* SILVIA.

YOLI   Mama!

SILVIA   Yoli!

They embrace. He attempts to pull her away but she does not leave.

CHORUS, GUESTS
    Libera de morte aeterna et lux aeterna luceat.

Small groups say goodbye and begin to walk away but then pause and continue talking, embracing, moving around restlessly, in circles.

Some lose the impulse to do anything, others become alarmed. Suddenly a flock of LAMBS *runs into the crowd.* LEONORA *and* LUCÍA *begin to pray. Armed* SOLDIERS *appear at the edge of the crowd in a bid to take control. Some people fail to notice that the cycle of inertia is slowly returning but several of the* GUESTS *realise the worst and react with horror: no one is able to leave the stage.*

Blackout.

END OF THE OPERA